Papier-Maché

This edition published 1977 by
Wayland (Publishers) Limited
49 Lansdowne Place, Hove, East Sussex BN3 1HF

SBN 85340 501 8

Filmset by Filmtype Services Limited, Scarborough
Printed in Italy by New Interlitho SpA

Beginning Crafts Series
created and produced by Sackett Publishing Services Ltd
2 Great Marlborough Street, London W1

Photography by Robert Glover Studios, Amersham, Bucks
Series Editor: Eve Harlow

Beginning Crafts

Papier-Maché

Charles Peattie

Illustrated by Frank Capon

Wayland Publishers England

Contents

The history of papier mâché

Papier mâché was invented in France in the reign of Louis XIV. Its invention was almost an accident. Parisians at that time loved going to plays and many rival theatre companies were formed. In order to attract audiences the theatres changed their programmes frequently and all over Paris posters were pasted up to advertise the current attractions. There was no time to peel one poster off a wall before another was stuck up with cow-heel glue, so the new one was simply stuck over the old, and very soon a thick pad of posters was stuck upon the wall.
A thrifty Parisian discovered that he could lever the pad off the wall, take it home, shape it, and smooth it and make it into trinket boxes which he painted and decorated and sold for good money. Soon others copied him.
The first man in England to use the new invention was a printer, John Baskerville. He decided to use panels made of papier mâché instead of wooden panels in building a coach for himself. As he pointed out to his friends, papier mâché was an ideal material because it was light yet resilient, strong and waterproof and could be moulded into the shape he wanted whereas wood had to be carved and bent.
Very soon afterwards a Birmingham businessman called Henry Clay invented a new improved way of making papier mâché which he called 'paperware'. Sheets of paper were stuck and pressed together, oiled, varnished and baked in an oven like china. In Clay's workshops women workers spent long hours rubbing the panels with pumice stone to get a really glossy surface ready for painting. At the end of the rubbing the papier mâché was as smooth as glass.
Clay started by making coach panels but soon he progressed to making trays, work-boxes and even chairs and tables. His goods were beautifully painted and decorated and were an instant success. Even though the prices were high, Clay's workshops could hardly keep up with the demand.
Eventually Clay's workshops were taken over by the famous firm of Jennens and Bettridge. By this time a new way of making papier mâché panels by compressing paper pulp in moulds under steam pressure was being used. Jennens & Bettridge were an adventurous and inventive firm. They discovered how to decorate papier mâché with an inlay of thin slivers of mother-of-pearl and, when the papier mâché chairs and tables proved too fragile to stand up to everyday wear and tear, they invented a method of covering stove-dried wooden frames with papier mâché to make the larger pieces of furniture.
In 1851 the Great Exhibition was held at Crystal Palace. Every kind of papier mâché furniture was on show including an entire bedroom suite and the case for a grand piano. Even a house was made from papier mâché.
Because it was so popular, other firms began to manufacture paperware goods. Many were shoddy and badly finished. In place of hand-painted flowers, the trays and tables were decorated with transfers which soon rubbed off. Soon nobody wanted papier mâché trays any more. The new craze was for silver-plated trays, made available by the invention of electro-plating late in the nineteenth century. The famous old firms closed down or were sold up and no-one made papier mâché commercially.
Papier mâché has revived as a handicraft because not only is newspaper cheap and easy to obtain but everyone wants to try and conserve raw materials and not simply burn waste paper. Papier mâché is an absorbing craft and covers a wide variety of techniques. You will find one that interests you in these pages and soon you will be able to make all kinds of attractive things – simply from paper, paste and paint.

Materials and tools

The most important factor in successful papier mâché is the choice of paper. For both layering and pulping, newspaper is the best paper to use because it absorbs the paste and becomes very soft and pliable.

Paper
Newspaper for layering should be torn into small pieces or, in some cases, into strips. The size of the pieces depends on the fineness of the modelling you are doing. A large flat surface needs pieces of about 60mm (2½in) square. For delicate modelling, as when making the features on puppet heads, tiny pieces the size of a fingernail are needed. When you are covering a curved surface like a balloon, tapering strips of newspaper 15–20mm (½–¾in) wide at the widest and 100mm (4in) long are the most successful. It is as well to tear up your paper in advance so that you are not delayed in your modelling. However, in doing fine work in modelling, it is more practical to tear each piece of paper individually to the approximate size that will fit into or around the object best. Never cut the paper with scissors – it will leave a hard line at the edge. A torn edge will blend onto the surface of your model and will not show.

Other types of paper
Normally it is best to avoid magazine paper or any paper with a shiny, water-repellant surface. However, you can give an interesting and attractive finish to a papier mâché bowl by using coloured paper from a magazine for the outermost layer. Tissue paper is absorbent, and layering or modelling with tissue paper gives a fine finish; it is, therefore, ideal for delicate work. Tissue paper can be purchased in many attractive colours. If you wish to be certain that you are layering evenly a useful method of keeping track is to use white and coloured paper for alternate layers. In the same way, coloured comics may be used in alternate layers with ordinary newsprint. Since tissue paper is so fine you may achieve an excellent finish by layering most of your model in newspaper but using tissue paper for the two outermost layers.

Paste
Besides paper, the other basic ingredient of papier mâché is paste. Paste is a cooked starch and water mixture which sets stiffly when it dries out. Wallpaper paste will make excellent papier mâché if you follow the directions on the packet. You can make flour and water paste as follows:

You will need:
A saucepan
A bowl
A spoon or metal whisk
1 cup of plain flour
2 pints of cold water
Oil of wintergreen or 1 tablespoon salt

Method
Put the flour in the pan. Gradually add the cold water, stirring all the time so that no lumps of dry flour are left in the mixture. A coiled wire whisk, such as is used to beat eggs or sauces, is useful for stirring. When all the water has been added to the flour, put the pan on the stove and bring the paste to the boil, stirring all the time. Cook until the paste turns translucent. Add a few drops of oil of wintergreen or a teaspoon of salt to prevent mould and fungus and allow to cool. If the paste is not for immediate use store in the refrigerator.

Methods in papier mâché
There are two methods of making a model in papier mâché; the first is the layering method, the second, the pulp method. Sometimes the two methods are combined in one model.
In the layering method small pieces or strips of paste-soaked paper are laid

onto the model to build up the thickness and shape required. Each layer is allowed to dry thoroughly before another is applied. In the pulp method, the pulp is moulded as if it were modelling clay, and then allowed to set in the shape you have made. Sometimes a model is built up round a mould which is later removed. At other times you will wish to build your model over a permanent frame or armature of wood, card or wire which forms a sort of skeleton for your model.

Pulping

To prepare newspaper for pulp, tear two double sheets of newspaper into shreds and soak it in a cup and a half of flour and water paste for about 30 minutes. At the end of this time, gather together the pulp and squeeze out the excess paste between your fingers.

Since paper is fibrous and is made from wood pulp, it is possible to disintegrate it and return it to the fibrous form by boiling it in water. A very fine smooth pulp may be made by gently boiling up three or four shredded sheets of newspaper, with just enough water to cover until the paper disintegrates. At this point, add one cup of flour mixed to a paste with water, to each quart of pulp and cook until it is thick enough to use.

A fine, even pulp can be made from paper handkerchiefs or table napkins or from 'Kleenex'-type toilet paper. Boil up a whole roll of paper (unrolled and squeezed down into the water).

Useful tools

Most tools used in papier mâché can be purchased at a model shop, including a polystyrene cutter and battery which powers it, and a crafts' knife. A crafts' knife is an effective instrument for precise cutting. To be so it has to be extremely sharp and should be treated with respect. Always stand the object to be cut on a cutting board and never cut towards your fingers.

Pliers and wire-cutters will be needed to make wire armatures. For card armatures, scissors and clear adhesive (for sticking dry paper) will be needed. A clear adhesive which sets quickly is more useful than ordinary gum.

TECHNIQUE AND PROJECT

Owl and pussycat

Pulp made with newspaper is fairly coarse and must be worked and squeezed in the hands to make it smooth. Paper pulp is a good modelling material and it can be used to make animal- and human-form models as long as the shape is fairly squat and has a flat base. It is possible to make very short legs on animal figures but they must be kept thick. To make a leg, break 3 or 4 matchsticks to about ¾ of the length. Push them together into the animal body while the pulp is still wet. Lay the animal on its back to dry. Paste paper strips over the legs to blend them into the body.

Small objects can be pushed into the animal models to suggest special features. Cloves make good giraffe horns for instance, ball-headed pins make bright noses, buttons can be used for eyes, string for tails, wool yarn for manes, etc.

Puppet heads

Marionette and puppet heads can be made with paper pulp. Model the pulp round a screwed up ball of paper or a roughly shaped modelling clay form. Make hand puppet heads over a piece of cardboard tube. When the head is joined to the glove body, the tube enables a finger to operate the head. Use ravelled string, scraps of wool yarn for eyebrows, hair and moustaches. These can be glued to the puppet heads after painting.

Materials, tools and equipment
Cup of flour and water paste, bowl
Newspaper, 2 sheets
Enamel, PVA or poster paints
A small sheet of polythene

Method
Put a cup-full (no more) of flour and water paste in a bowl and add two, or perhaps more, sheets of newspaper shredded into 12mm (½in) strips. Leave the shreds to soak and absorb the paste **(1)**.
Gather the pulp into a lump in your hand and squeeze out the excess paste through your fingers until you have formed a rough ball **(2)**.
Dump the ball firmly onto a sheet of polythene to flatten the base, then with the fingers, shape the lump into a rough pear-shape with a slight curve inwards for the cat's neck. Make another lump for the owl.
To make the ears of the cat and the horns and beak of the owl, pinch and pat the pulp into shape with your fingers **(3)**. If there are any obvious cracks in the pulp, cover them with small pieces of paste-soaked paper.
Allow the models to dry thoroughly in a warm place, then paint them with acrylic or PVA paint or emulsion paint or with very thick poster paint. Draw the faces, paws, wings, feathers etc., with a paint brush or felt pen. Varnish the models if poster paint is used **(4)**.

PROJECT

Scorpion brooch

Having successfully modelled paper pulp into solid shapes, the next stage is building up relief areas on a base. If the mixture is squeezed and worked until all the lumps are smoothed out, modelling with paper pulp is very satisfying and good effects can be achieved. Small projects, such as the scorpion brooch illustrated (it is about 70mm (3in) long), need very fine-grained pulp. Instead of newspaper, use tissue paper. Cheap toilet rolls provide a lot of paper of the right weight. Tear small pieces – about the size of postage stamps, and soak the paper in paste for several hours.

Tips on modelling
Use your fingers first to achieve the general shape. Smooth the surface and then use a tool to model the details. Use sharpened matchsticks, the flat end of an orange stick, a pencil point, a small knife tip, hair grips etc.

Texturing
Shapes can be textured to represent fur, feathers or scales. The end of a wire hairpin could be used to make fish scales for instance. Experiment with things like old toothbrushes to see what textural effects you can make.

Decorating
The scorpion brooch is painted red all over with the details picked out in black. This has produced a bright, bold effect. Try painting stripes on the body, or add beads for a glittering lapel pin.

Materials, tools and equipment
Thin card
Scissors
Thin paper, paste
Newspaper
Clear adhesive
Modelling tool of some kind
Bright red paint, black ink or paint
Brushes, varnish
Safety pin, clear adhesive tape

Method
Make paper pulp with thin paper pieces and paste. Leave to soak. Draw the scorpion shape on card. Give it a forward curling tail. You need not draw in the front legs or the side legs. Paste paper strips over the card to make a surface for the pulp. While the surface is still wet, spoon pulp on the card shape **(1)**. Model with the fingers first to get the general shape. Work the details with a tool **(2)**. Add pieces of paper to look like the carapace (shell) if you like. Tear strips of newspaper to make the heavy front legs and the thinner side legs. Fold strips lengthwise and then twist in the middle, pinching the ends to make points **(3)**. Leave the legs to dry. Glue legs to the body and then paint red all over **(4)**. Paint in the details in black. Tape a large safety pin to the back of the brooch to make a fastening **(5)**. If you are using poster paints for decorating, remember that a coat of varnish helps to keep the colour permanent. A variety of brooches can be made in the same way **(6)**.

Bangles

The bangles are made by modelling pulp onto a cardboard base to build up a rounded surface.

Materials, tools and equipment
Thin card
Pulp made from paste and newspaper
Newspaper strips, paste
String for decoration
Contact adhesive
Paints, brushes, varnish

Method
Cut a strip of thin card about 38mm (1½in) wide and long enough so that it will pass over your knuckles when it is formed into a ring. Add 25mm (1in) to the length for overlap **(1)**. Glue the ends together with contact adhesive **(2)**.
Bind the bangle with strips of paste-soaked paper so that it has a smooth even surface **(3)**. Allow to dry.
With pulp, thicken the band so that a cross-section would look like a segment of an orange with the outer curve away from your wrist. Bind again with one layer of paper **(4)**.
To decorate, cover the outer surface of the bangle with glue and press a length of string onto the glue in a wavy design. It is easier if you stick the string on bit by bit – about 25mm (1in) at a time **(5)**.
When this has dried, paint the bangle to match your dress. To make the string pattern stand out, allow the first coat of paint to dry, then take a brush covered with a lighter shade of fairly thick paint. Brush lightly over the string so that the paint sticks to the raised surface **(6)**.
When thoroughly dry, finish the bangle with a single coat of varnish.

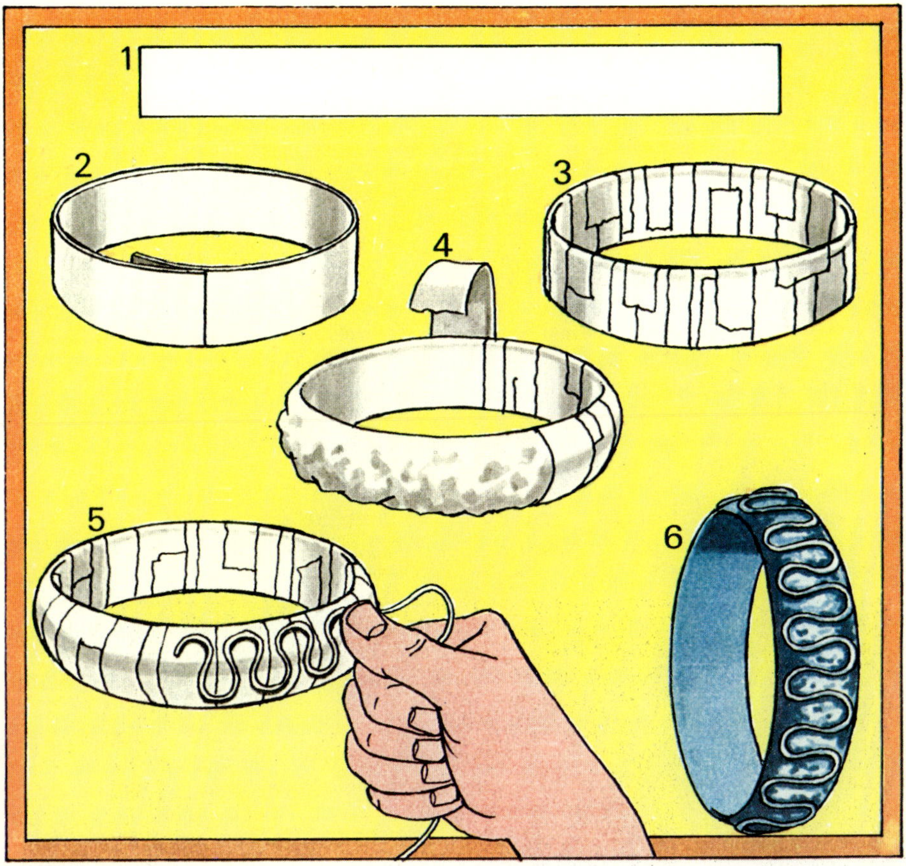

Decorating ideas
Twist thin strips of tissue paper into ropes and glue them to the finished jewellery after painting. Varnish. Make 'jewels' by screwing balls of tissue paper and covering them with circles of tissue. Flatten the balls and glue to the bracelet. Varnish afterwards. Pieces of pasta (the decoratively shaped varieties) can be glued in patterns and painted in bright colours.
Stage jewellery of all kinds is made in the same way as the bracelets. Crowns for kings and queens, big brooches for cloaks, military orders, pendant jewels, belt and shoe buckles and of course, bracelets of all kinds. Swords and daggers, made of heavy cardboard and silver-painted, can be given jewelled handles. Be-jewelled drinking cups for feast and banquet scenes can be made from spray-painted plastic cups.

Brooches and pendants Cut card to shapes. Cover with paper strips. Model settings in pulp or glue string in patterns. Push bits of pulp in between some of the string patterns. Or decorate with pasta shapes. Paint with poster colours or PVA colours. Pick out the decorations in silver, gold or in contrasting colours. Sprinkle glitter dust onto wet glue, or group small beads and sequins.

Crowns Cut strips of card about 150mm (6in) deep and long enough to fit the head when the ends are overlapped. Draw diamond points or scallops along the top edge and cut out. Join the ends with sticky tape or glue. Model pulp to resemble gold settings for jewels. Spray gold or silver. Make jewels from pulp or tissue paper or glue big beads to the crowns.

Patriotic hat

Here layering is worked over a framework of strips. If you find paper strips difficult to control, use thin card. The big brim of the hat is based on a piece of card but there is another method by which large areas of papier mâché can be built up. It is similar to the original papier mâché method which was used to form coach panels and table tops.

The method You need 10–12 sheets of a large-sized newspaper and wallpaper paste. Smooth the first sheet flat and paste it all over, right to the edges. Carefully smooth the next sheet on top of the paste, pressing out air bubbles. Creases do not matter. Paste again and spread another sheet of newspaper on top. Continue pasting and papering until the wad is as thick as you need. Leave the wad to dry. When it is still moist and yet can be handled, the papier mâché can be cut into shapes with a crafts' knife or moulded over a form. You can make a tray, for instance, by oiling the surface and then pressing a wad of papier mâché to the shape. You may need to cut slits in the edges to get a good fit. Leave to dry. Remove and make a form of the other side of the tray. Join top and bottom with pasted paper strips. Sandpaper to smooth the surface and paint.

A big-brimmed hat to make and wear for a parade!

Materials, tools and equipment
Card for the base
2 piles of books and two sticks about 610mm (24in) long
Newspaper, paste and paint

Method
Cut a disc of card about 46cm (1½ft) in diameter **(1)**. Cut a hole to fit the crown of your head **(2)**. Try the brim on your head to see whether it fits. It should be a little bit loose to allow for the layering.
Lay the brim upon two sticks across two piles of books. All round the edge of the inner brim paste 25mm (1in) wide strips of pasted paper. Paste all of the strips, both sides **(3)**. Each strip should be roughly 300mm (12in) long. Allow the strips to hang down through the hole and dry so that they become stiff **(4)**.
Tear 50mm (2in) wide strips of paper. Paste the strips and wind them horizontally round the hanging strips, drawing them together to form the crown **(5)**. Leave to dry.
Turn the hat over. Paste wider strips across the crown of the hat. Add an extra layer of papier mâché beyond the outside of the brim to make it slightly wavy. Layer all over the brim and crown to give the hat a better finish **(6)**.
When the hat is thoroughly dry, paint it in a pattern in the colours of the national flag **(7)**.

PROJECT

Mammoth relief

Relief modelling can also be used to make dramatic wall panels. A really big panel might become a group project.

Materials, tools and equipment

1 sheet of hardboard about 510mm × 760mm (20in × 30in)
Quantity of prepared paper pulp
Emulsion paint, white
Paints, brushes, varnish
Large paint-brush
Indelible felt-tipped pen
Newspaper, paste

Method

Paint the sheet of hardboard with emulsion paint so that it does not absorb the paste.

Draw the outline of the mammoth on the board with an indelible felt pen **(1)**.

Start modelling by working inside the drawn line with large lumps of pulp – whole sheets of newspaper soaked and squeezed together build up quickly **(2)**. The thickest pad of pulp will be at the shoulders and flanks of the animal. There will be indentations to model the eye, round the back and behind the forelegs. Completely fill the outline with pulp but taper it off towards the edges. Build up the mountains too with pulp.

When you have completed the modelling, cover the parts of the board which are not hidden by pulp with a single layer of pasted paper. This gives a good surface for painting.

To make the tusks smooth model the shape first with pulp, then cover with a

layer of pasted strips **(3)**. The rest of the animal requires a rougher surface – remember mammoths were shaggy animals!
Allow everything to dry thoroughly – this may take several days – and then paint your relief picture **(4)**.

Ideas to try
Relief pictures look very exciting if the background surface is textured. Try the effect of sprinkled sand or press bracken leaves into the wet emulsion paint. The paint will hold the bracken as it dries. The leaves might be arranged as a forest background to an animal.
Several people can work on a large relief modelling project. An underwater scene for instance with a variety of fantastic fish and monsters, or a jungle scene with leaves, bushes, snakes and wild animals, make suitable large panel themes.

Relief abstracts
Abstract themes are fascinating to work in paper. Use pulp, paper strips, pieces of corrugated card, pleated paper, thick card torn into pieces etc., to build up a design. Strips of thick and thin card, glued together in a haphazard fashion, pieces of string, smooth and thin, hairy sisal, bits of rope can be added for texture and contrast. Paint the finished picture in a plain, matt colour.

Portraits in relief
Try making a relief portrait sculpture. Sit your model with a light behind him. Hold a piece of paper in front of him so that his shadow falls on the paper. Trace round the outline of his profile. Draw the profile onto a prepared board. Apply pulp inside the outline, smoothing the pulp towards the edges. Model features using fingers and a tool for finer details. Paint the background black and the sculpture white.

PROJECT

Baroque vanity mirror

Turn an ordinary handmirror into a glamorous looking gift. You can use the same technique to make old frames look like gilt frames.

Materials, tools and equipment
Handmirror with a wood frame (or a handbag mirror and a stiff card mount)
Prepared paper pulp
Modelling tool (optional)
Spray paint, gold or silver
Newspaper, paste

Method
Use an ordinary wood-framed hand-mirror or mount a handbag mirror or an old oval mirror to a stiff card mirror shape **(1)**. Paste strips of paper all over the wood (or card) to make a surface for the pulp. Cover the back of the mirror with pulp first. Model and tool it **(2)**. Try simple lines from side to side or a spiral swirl. Leave face down until dry. Now work the front of the mirror, working pulp up to the mirror edge carefully and blending the front and back on the mirror edges. Mask the mirror surface with paper and tape **(3)**. Paint the pulp with black first and then spray with gold or silver (or any colour preferred). Plain wood picture frames can be made to look like gilt frames with paper pulp designs and a coat of gold paint **(4)**.
In this project, papier mâché pulp is used to add moulding to an object. There is almost no end to the uses of

paper pulp for this purpose as long as the object is properly prepared with pasted paper strips. The surface to be worked must be roughened so that the pulp sticks. Polished wood should be sanded down with coarse paper.

Ideas for pulp decoration

Picture frames are fairly easy to decorate. You can make pulp moulding look like an ornate carved frame, adding string or beads to make stems and flowers. Glue pieces of thin rope round the inside edge of a frame, butting the cut ends in corners. Work pulp from the rope to the outer edge of the frame in a smooth curve. Paint the frame gold – it should look like a beaded frame. You can make frames from stiff cardboard and build up the pulp decoration. By adding twisted strips of tissue paper, scrolls and frond effects could be made.

Pulp will stick to wood furniture too. Try making claw and ball feet for an old chair or build up the back of an ordinary kitchen chair to make a curved effect. Paper pulp makes a good foundation for hand-painting and you could try painting garlands of flowers across the chair back.

Box lids will take a pulped decoration. Make sure that the pulp is smoothed right to the edges of the lid.

TECHNIQUE AND PROJECT

Layering in papier mâché is a technique by which pieces of paper are pasted to a form to build up a surface which can then be painted or decorated. Layering is sometimes combined with pulp to produce three dimensional effects.

Tips on layering

Newspaper is the best paper for most projects (see page 6). Tear up sufficient paper before you begin pasting. It is better to have too much than to have to stop pasting, wash your hands and start tearing in the middle of a project. Always tear paper – never cut it. Torn edges produce a smoother finish.

Have a bowl of clean water nearby and rinse your fingers often. If you are using salt as a preservative (page 6) it is better to clean off the paste from time to time because salt has a drying effect on the skin and your fingers are likely to become sore.

How to paste strips

Pick up a strip between forefinger and thumb. Dip it in the paste, slide the forefinger and thumb of the other hand down the strip to remove the surplus paste, smooth the strip on to the object. Never leave strips soaking in the paste because they will become too sodden to use.

Applying strips

One layer of strips dries in about an hour. If you are working on a piece that is to have 6–8 layers, apply 2 or 3 and leave to dry overnight before applying the next 2–3 layers.

Try to allow sufficient time for papier mâché to dry naturally. It can be dried artificially, in an oven or near to a heater, but this quite often results in shrinkage and distortion.

Matchbox doorstop

Any stone will make a doorstop as long as it can be layered to smooth off sharp edges. A round or oval stone needs papering only so that it can be decorated – to look like a curled, sleeping cat for instance.

Papier mâché doorstops should not be decorated with pulp. It is liable to get knocked off by passers by.

Try other designs which lend themselves to an oblong shape. A soldier standing to attention perhaps or a skyscraper with rows of lit windows.

Materials, tools and equipment
A clean brick
Prepared pulp
Newspaper
Paste
Sandpaper
PVA paints or poster colours and varnish
Brushes, felt-tipped pen
Piece of felt

Method
Find a brick, wash and dry it thoroughly. Fill the cavity with paper pulp to level the top **(1)**.
Cover the brick entirely with large pieces of paste-soaked paper. This will protect your doorstop from grazing or chipping. Four layers should be enough **(2)**.
When thoroughly dry, sandpaper smooth. Paint with emulsion paint **(3)**. Draw a line all the way round the brick threequarters of the way along. This marks off the outside of the box from the 'drawer'. Paint the sides of the brick to the three-quarter line. Paint the flat top of the brick to represent the outside of a matchbox and paint the remainder to look like the open drawer containing matches. Glue felt on base.

PROJECT

Relief map

Making a relief map is a good way of learning to read contour maps. If you were on a trek in a strange country, it would be important to be able to recognize the terrain around you from a map. On maps, steep mountains are shown with the contour lines close together. You would be able to choose an easier route by spotting a place where the contour lines were wide apart and the ground therefore gently sloping. Relief maps can be included in a geography project. Display photographs and maps of the area.

Colouring relief maps
When colouring the map, choose realistic colours – dark green for forested areas, lighter green for lowlands, white for mountain peaks etc. Alternatively, paint in the same colours as a contour map – white at the peaks, mauve lower down and pale green in the valleys.

Realistic models
It can be fun to make a really large relief map, with lakes, rivers and perhaps a sea shore and put in the trees and forests. Cotton wool dipped in thick, green poster paint and allowed to dry, makes bushes and trees. Glue the wool to twigs to make copses and forests. You might show rivers with a reflective material such as foil paper. By strewing gravel onto a glue-smeared surface, you can make very realistic-looking textured areas.

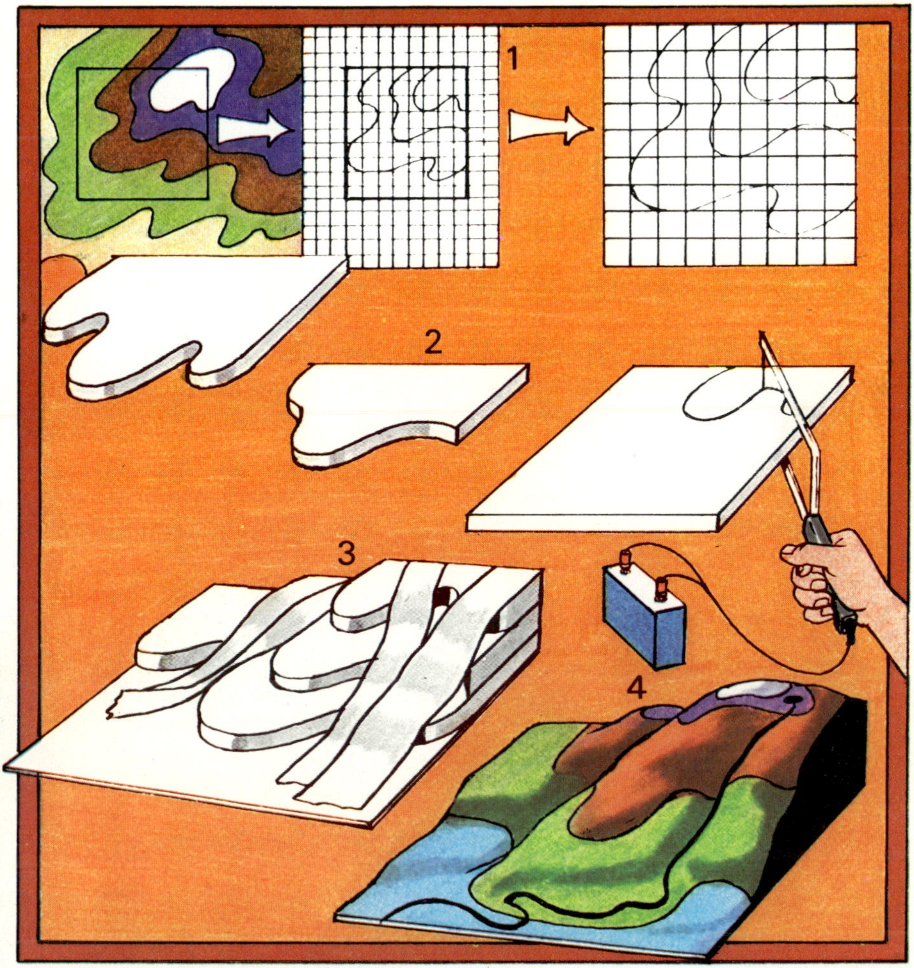

Materials, tools and equipment
Hardboard base
5 polystyrene tiles, paints
Polystyrene tile cutter and battery
Newspaper and paste

Method
Choose a hilly section of a contour map. Mark the square to be modelled. Trace the contour lines in the square and transfer the tracing onto squared paper. By marking another sheet of paper into larger squares you can enlarge the tracing of your contour shape ready for the model **(1)**. Trace each contour line onto a separate polystyrene tile and cut round the lines with the tile cutter **(2)**.
Using thick flour and water paste or special polystyrene tile glue, stick the lowest contour line onto the hardboard base, the next above it, and so on to the highest line **(3)**.

Important: Do not use any other type of glue. Many adhesives dissolve polystyrene tiles. Allow tiles to dry then cover the slopes with long strips of pasted newspaper, allowing each layer to dry before applying the next. Two layers should be sufficient. Paint the model **(4)**.

Chessmen

Making figures over cardboard tubes is a technique which can be adapted for all kinds of characters. Once you have mastered the basic structure and you have understood how to make the heads and shoulders, you will be able to invent different effects. Try the Bishop first (instructions on page 26), this is the simplest structure. Tall cardboard tubes that held coloured, chocolate beans were used for the chessmen.

Dressing figures
Two methods are used for giving the robes realistic-looking folds. In one, rolls of paper are pasted to the figure and strips are pasted over the top. The other way – which needs practising – involves soaking large pieces of paper in paste, then draping the paper over the figure, pushing the folds into the paper with the thumbs. Figures can have other things added to the robes. Glue on pieces of gold foil, scraps of lace paper, sequins, pretty buttons, beads, motifs cut from magazines. Cut pieces from bendy white card and paint them to look like shields, swords, daggers etc.

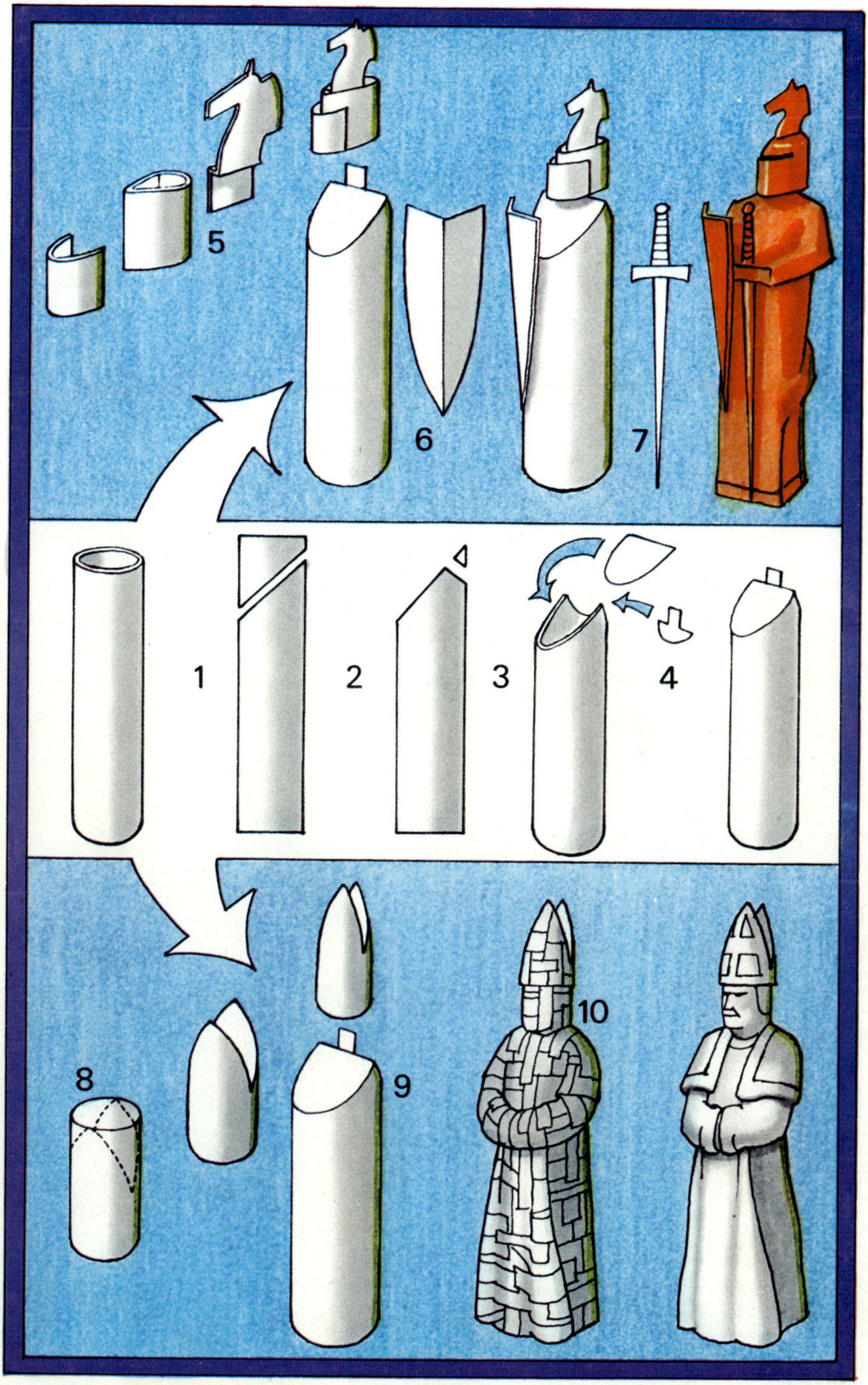
5
6
7
1
2
3
4
8
9
10

1
2
3
4
5
6
7
8
9
10

Making the chessmen

Materials, tools and equipment
4 tall cardboard tubes, 152mm to 203mm (6in to 8in) tall
Thin, pliable card
Newspaper
Paste
Tissue paper
Scissors, crafts' knife
Emulsion paint
Enamel paints, brushes
Black ink and pen for details

Method

Knight and Bishop (see page 25)
The body structure for both figures is worked in the same way. Cut a segment of the tube off at an angle **(1)**. Cut a further segment from the back **(2)**. From the card, cut pieces to fit the chest and the back neck **(3)**. The neck-piece should have a tab **(4)**. Fit a circle of card in the base of the tube, first putting in a coin to weight the tube.
For the Knight, make a cylinder of card for the helmet and add a curved visor. Cut out a horse's head crest and glue this to the top of the helmet **(5)**. Cut a shield shape. Fold it vertically **(6)**. Cut a sword. Assemble pieces on the figure **(7)**.
For the Bishop, cut a cylinder deep enough to be both the face and the hat. Shape the top to a mitre **(9)**. Glue the cylinder to the neck tab. The figures are now ready for layering **(10)**.
Queen and King (see opposite)
The Queen and King are made on the same basic body structure.
For the Queen, cut a piece from a cylinder **(1)**. Cut a square of card for the shoulders **(2)**. Make small cylinders for the head and neck **(3)**. Trim the smaller tube at an angle. Cut a curved piece for the collar **(4)**. Assemble the pieces – the head leans back from the body. Layer, add the folds and layer to finish.
For the King, make the head lean forward. Cut the top of the tube at an angle **(6)**. Cut a piece of card for the shoulder 'table' **(7)**. Cut and make a cylinder for the head and crown. Glue to the shoulder table **(8)**.

Finishing all figures
Using small strips of newspaper, layer all over the figures to cover the added pieces and round-off the joins **(9)**. Quite a lot of layering is needed to build up the shoulders and arms of the Queen and King **(10)**. Finish with small pieces of a thinner paper to make a good surface for painting. Paint with emulsion paint first and then with enamel paints to decorate. Add details in black ink.

Ideas for figures
Beautiful figures for Christmas can be made on the same principle. Make the Virgin in blue and white, Joseph in brown and black, and dress the Kings in brilliant colours. Alternatively, paint the figures entirely in gold. Make a group of figures from history, kings and queens, cardinals and warriors. Make a group of costumed people from other nations, dressing them in their national costumes. Make a collection of soldiers in uniforms from through the ages. Always try to keep the clothes simple in line but build up the shape with layering under the final layer.

Wobbling clowns

The technique described for making the clowns achieves a very fine finish in papier mâché. By applying white tissue paper to a finished piece you can make the surface absolutely smooth – smooth enough to paint on it in water-colours. But it takes time to do properly. Every layer must be perfectly applied and left to dry before putting on the next. An even better surface can be achieved with gesso powder. This is a white, chalk-like substance. Mix it with water to a smooth paste and smear it over the surface. When it is dry, smooth it down with a fine-grade sandpaper and then cover with gesso again. The finished surface is rather like porcelain. Gesso is particularly good for filling in cracks but of course, creases in the paper should be sanded smooth.

Materials, tools and equipment
An egg
Contact adhesive, lead shot
Thin paper, white tissue paper, paste
Oil paints or poster paints and varnish

Method
The egg must be blown first. To do this, pierce a tiny hole in each end using a needle point, then the eye end. Put your mouth to one hole and gently blow the contents out through the other hole into a bowl. Wash the eggshell carefully in warm water. Allow to dry **(1)**. Layer with very small pieces

of paper, leaving the hole at the pointed end of the egg uncovered **(2)**. Dry between each layer. After 3 layers drip a small amount of clear adhesive in through the hole so that it drops on the bottom of the inside **(3)**.
Immediately drop in a tiny lead shot so that it lands on the glue **(4)**. Allow the glue to dry.
Add 2–3 more layers of paper, covering the hole **(5)**.
Finish layering with two layers of white tissue paper, carefully applied to avoid creasing. When dry, paint the egg **(6)**. Stand the egg clown on a table and push him over with your finger. He will wobble but will always return upright.

Egg-bird mobile
This is another way of using eggshells as a base. Blow several eggs or collect eggshell halves and glue them together. Cover the surface with tiny pieces of soft white paper. Build up about 4 layers. Add a 5th layer, working from the blunt end towards the pointed end. Leave one edge of paper free and unpasted. Collect some white, fluffy chicken feathers. Glue one to each side of the egg for wings. Glue a small bunch to the pointed end for a tail. Brush yellow or blue paint over the body. Paint black eyes. Thread black cotton right through the body on a long needle. Tie the thread ends to a mobile.

Candlestick

Another simple project using layering over a permanent base – in this case, glass jars. Making candlesticks could be a wonderful group project. Everyone could collect small jars of different shapes and then make candlesticks for Christmas decorations or for a bazaar.

Materials, tools and equipment
3 clean small jars or pots, ie, yeast extract, mustard, babyfood or cosmetic jars
Masking tape
String
Contact adhesive
Newspaper, paste
Paints, brushes
Modelling clay for a weight

Method
Choose one of the jars to be the base and fill with bits of modelling clay to weight it and give the candlestick stab-

ility. Put the lid on. Spread glue on the lid. Stand the next jar on top with its lid on. Glue the lid. The topmost jar should have the smallest mouth so that it will take a candle. Strengthen the joins with two bands of tape **(1)**.
Layer all over the candlestick, taking the layers over the rim of the top jar. Keep paper pieces small so that the shape of the jars can still be seen. Dry between each layer. Four layers will be enough **(2)**. The candlestick is now ready for decorating **(3)**.

Decorating ideas
Take a 250mm (10in) piece of string and coil it round as if you were making a flat coil of rope. This can most easily be done between your fingers. Smear the area of the candlestick to be decorated with contact adhesive and press the coil against the glue.
Allow to dry, paint the stick and insert a candle. The candlestick illustrated was painted red, and then gold paint was brushed onto some areas to give an 'antique' look **(4)**.

Appliqué decoration Cut-outs of thick card, glued to the sides of the stick, can be painted in a contrast colour. Cut stars, moons, diamonds etc. Glue dried leaves to the candlestick after painting. Paint with polyurethane varnish. Cut shapes from coloured foils to fit the facets of the jars. Paste thin strips of black paper over the foil to make window shapes.

Nativity candlesticks
By glueing a small jar on top of a tall jar and weighting the base, candlesticks could be papered and decorated to simulate the robes of the Three Kings. The small jar could form the head of the figure, the candle fitting into this jar. Paint the robes in brilliant colours and add beads and sequins for jewellery. Paint the small jar with features, long hair, beard and moustache.

Maracas

Layering over an inflated balloon means that you can make a round, hollow shell. The balloon is burst and taken out of the shell after the papier mâché is dry. All kinds of things can be made from a complete sphere: a piggy bank, for instance, by adding 4 squat feet made from wound, pasted strips and a flat nose made from 8–9 circles of paper pasted together. Cut a slit in the pig's back for the money.

A sphere will also make a pretty hanging basket. Cut round holes in the sides and pierce small holes near the rim for the hanging cords. Cut the top off. Paint the shell inside and out with two coats of emulsion paint and then two coats of gloss paint. Decorate with patterns or motifs. Fill with soil and plant trailing flowers in the holes. Hang from a plaited cord.

Masks are easy to make on an inflated balloon. Rest the balloon in a basin and paper about half way down. Paste a cone of paper in the middle for a nose. Give the mask about 6 layers, lift off the balloon and cut two eye holes. Paint the mask, pierce two holes on the edge for ties.

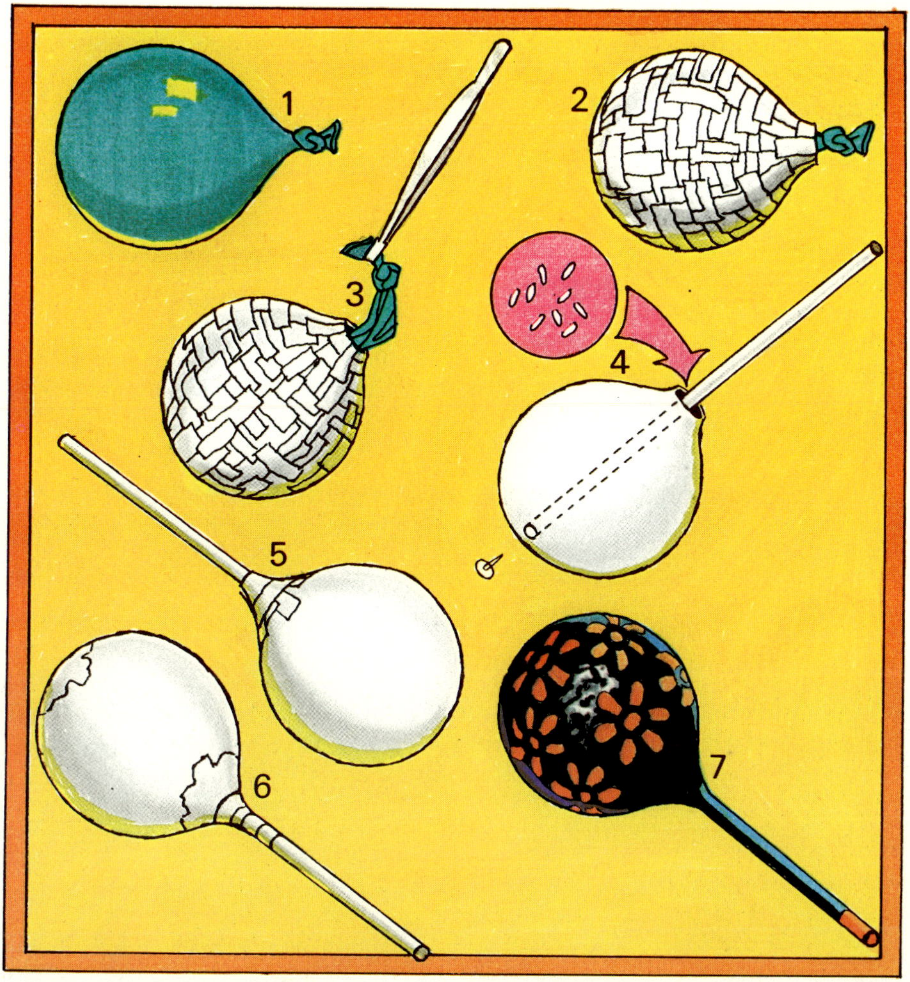

Materials, tools and equipment
2 balloons (and a spare for accidents)
Soft paper, paste
2 pieces of wood, 250mm (10in) long, 12mm (½in) thick
Lentils, split peas or rice for filling
2 thumb tacks, tweezers

Method
Blow up the balloons to 127mm (5in) diameter **(1)**. Cover with oil, using the hands.

Give each balloon four layers of tiny pieces of torn paper no wider than 25mm (1in) **(2)**. Leave a small hole around the balloon knot. Allow the maracas to dry between each layer but do not put them in a warm place to dry as the balloon will probably expand in the warmth and burst. When the paper is dry, burst the balloons through the hole and pull them out with tweezers **(3)**.

Trickle a few lentils or grains of rice in through the hole. Push a length of wood through the hole in the shell until it touches the end. Push a thumb tack through the shell and into the wood, to hold it in place **(4)**.

Close the gap round the wood with strips of pasted paper **(5)**. Layer over the head of the thumb tack **(6)**.

Paint and decorate the finished maracas with bright colours **(7)**.

Devil mask

Materials, tools and equipment
Balloon, pot or basin, oil
Newspaper, paste, paint
Clear adhesive tape,

Method
Inflate the balloon to the size of your own head. Cover it with a film of oil. Stand it on a flower pot or a basin with the knot downwards. Draw a horizontal line round the balloon about half way down **(1)**.
Layer down to the line with 4 layers **(2)**. When dry, trim edge, remove from balloon **(3)**. From thin card cut nose-shape with a tab at the upper end and use this to attach it to the dome **(4)**. Stand the dome on a table-top, one half projecting over the edge. Fasten to the table with pieces of tape **(5)**
On each side of the dome, paste two double strips of newspaper about 50mm (2in) wide. These will hang down on either side of the eyes. Join the strips to the nose below the eyes. Allow to dry.
Suspend further strips from the horizontal band below the eyes and from the nose. Using your hand to model against, join the hanging strips with a layer of pasted pieces to form the lower half of the face. Leave to dry **(6)**.
Build up the cheeks, eyebrows and chin with pulp. For the lips, roll up two 76mm (3in) cylinders of paste-soaked paper, and stick these to the base **(7)**. They will be squashed slightly as you stick them on, which is a good thing. Make cones of pasted newspaper for horns **(8)**. Layer round the horns to

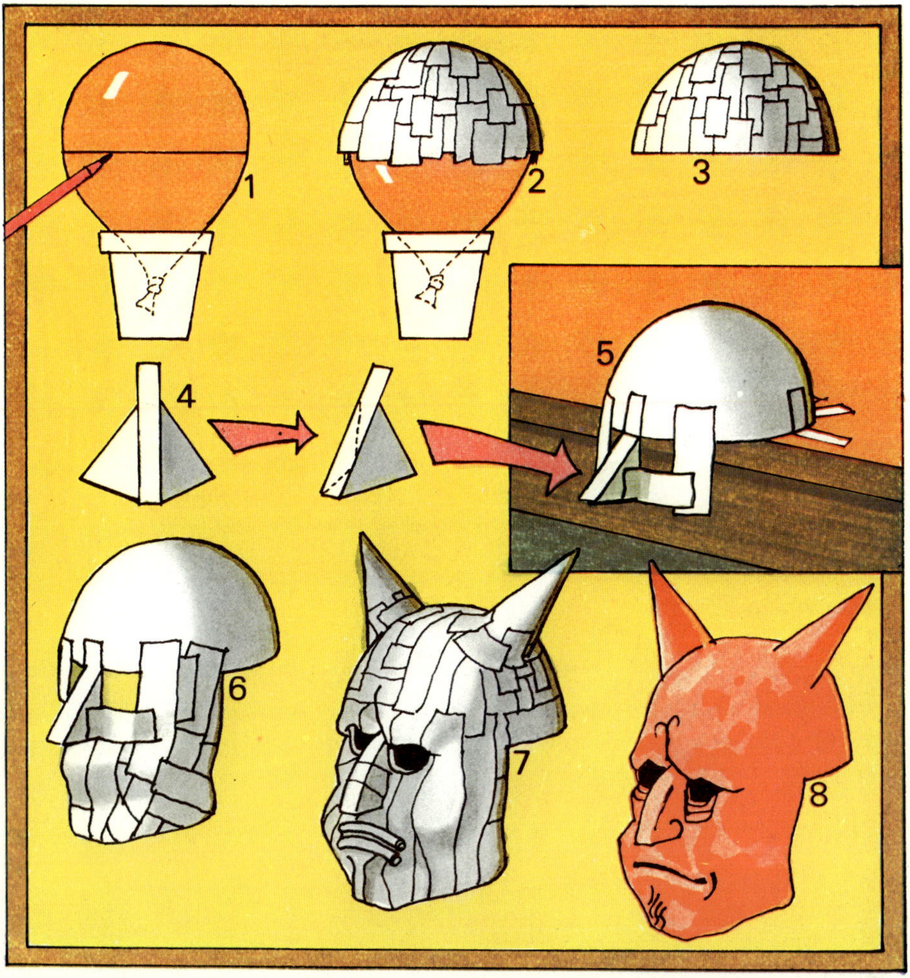

secure them. Layer over the pulp areas. Paint.

This mask is rather a complicated structure but it is a good project for building up a shape in paper. You can see that once you have made the solid dome, the rest of the head can be hung downwards from this.

Quite large mask heads could therefore be made on the same principle. If the dome were made on a large, round bowl, for instance, a carnival mask head of up to 915mm (36in) in diameter could be built on it. It would be difficult to make it strong enough working only in paper. The hanging strips would be better, therefore, in a lightweight card, fastened in position with a strong adhesive. When the basic framework is made, use pasted newspaper strips to build up the features and to join structures. For the final, outer layer of paper, use thin brown wrapping paper, glueing it to the newspaper. Spray-paint the head. You will probably need to wrap the lower edge of the head with several layers of paper strips.

Tips on spray-painting Spray paint dries very quickly but if you are not very careful it paints everything else around you at the same time. Paint outside in the open if you can. Arrange a screen of sheets of newspaper over cardboard boxes so that the object you are painting is protected on three sides. Then start spraying.

Bowls and dishes

You can make a whole set of bowls or dishes from one mould. Remember that papier mâché should not be washed. The finished surface is reasonably waterproof and the dishes can be used for semi-wet foods but they should be cleaned by wiping with a wet cloth and dried immediately.

Materials, tools and equipment
Bowl or dish
Vegetable oil or cling-wrap film
Soft paper in two colours
Tissue paper
Flour and water paste
Crafts' knife
Palette knife
Gesso powder
Emulsion paint
Paints, brushes

Method
Turn the bowl upside down. Cover the outside with vegetable oil, using the hands, or with a carefully smoothed-on layer of cling-wrap **(1)**.
Layer with tiny pieces of soft paper. Work each layer in a different colour so that you can see that you have covered the whole bowl. It is important that the papier mâché is of the same thickness all over. Take great care to avoid creases and allow the bowl to dry

thoroughly between each layer **(2)**. Finish with 2–3 layers of tissue paper and then 2 coats of gesso.
Paint the outside of the bowl **(3)** with emulsion paint and allow to dry. Ease the shell off the mould with the aid of a palette knife **(4)**. To do this slide the knife up between the papier mâché and the mould, then ease it round until the paper bowl comes loose.
Trim the rim of the bowl with a crafts' knife so that it is even **(5)**. It may need sandpapering to get a smooth edge. Paint both the outside and inside of the bowl and when the paint is dry, decorate it **(6)**.
More complicated shapes can be reproduced in papier mâché by covering the whole of the utensil with paper. To make a vase, for instance, oil the surface first and then cover it with up to 8 layers of paper. Leave to dry thoroughly. Mark the central line from the rim to the base on two sides. Using a crafts' knife and with someone else holding the vase, cut carefully along the line. It is better to make several light cuts than to try and cut through the papier mâché in one go. Lift the two halves from the vase. Neaten the edges and join them together again with pasted strips of paper. Cover the whole shape with tissue paper layers and finish with two or three coats of gesso.

Decorating ideas Hand-painted decorations look most effective on papier mâché pots and dishes but if you cannot draw or paint, use transfers or cutouts from magazines or catalogues. Flower heads, cut from a seedsman's catalogue would look very effective, grouped or arranged in a free design. Give paste-ons or transfers two or three coats of varnish to finish.

Gift egg or jewel box

Pretty gift 'eggs' are easily made on a fruit base – the fruit is perfectly alright to eat afterwards. If you want to make a larger egg – use a melon! Line gift eggs with pasted scraps of pretty gift paper. If you choose the paper carefully, you should be able to achieve a 'confetti' effect. Decorate the outsides of eggs by first painting and then adding cut-out initials, motifs, scraps of silver paper lace, etc.

Materials, tools and equipment

An orange, grapefruit or an old rubber ball
Newspaper and coloured magazine pages
Flour and water paste, oil or polythene film
Crafts' knife, sandpaper
Paints, brushes
Lace trims, paper lace, silver paper lace, foil, coloured cellophane etc

Method

Cover the mould with vegetable oil **(1)** or cling wrap film **(2)**. You will find it easier to work if you balance the mould on a cup or bowl and cover first one half, then turn the mould over and cover the other half. Layer with small pieces of paper carefully avoiding creases. First make a layer with plain newspaper, then allow it to dry. Use coloured comic paper for the next

layer, and continue using plain and coloured paper alternately for about ten layers. This allows you to be sure that you have covered the mould evenly **(3)**.

Before you remove the shell from the mould, give it one coat of paint **(4)**. This helps to avoid the possibility of warping. Draw a straight line round the widest part of the egg. Taking care not to slice your finger, cut along the line with a crafts' knife so that the egg is in two halves **(5)**. Ease the egg off the mould. Sandpaper the edges until they are absolutely smooth. Paint the inside and out.

A pretty edging can be made by sticking a narrow band of lace round the inner rims of the eggs using contact adhesive **(6)**. Decorate by painting and glueing on trims and motifs.

Jewel boxes

Make a large egg on a grapefruit or a melon. Make a hinge for the two halves with fabric adhesive tape. Use two pieces, one inside, the other outside. Paint or line the inside of the egg. Give the outside two coats of emulsion paint. Glue three paper balls to the underside of the egg for feet. Paint the outside in a bright, jewel colour. Glue a strip of gold or silver paper lace round the upper and lower rims. Give the finished egg at least 3 coats of varnish on the outside. You might decorate the top of the jewel box with a beautiful button or a group of glittering beads.

Toby jug

Toby Jugs are old English pottery and always look like an old man sitting.

Materials, tools and equipment
Plastic tub, paper pulp, newspaper
Emulsion paint, paints, varnish

Method
Paint the tub all over with emulsion paint or cover with paper strips **(1)**. Stick on a lump of pulped newspaper to form the nose, another for the chin, two smaller lumps for the cheeks and a horizontal projection for the brow. Starting on a line with the cheeks, on each side of the tub model shoulders and arms with the hands resting on the knee lumps. Add the feet. To make the lumps stay in position, cover each with a piece of paste-soaked paper, large enough to cover the projection and extend over the flat surface of the tub. Leave to dry **(2)**. For the handle, roll a paste-soaked piece of paper, bend it into shape, squeeze the lower end flat against the mug and fasten it on with a paper strip. Bend the top end of the handle round and fasten it with a strip, underneath the rim with the end pointing downward **(3)**.
Cover the tub both inside and out with a layer of paper pieces. Build up the rim to shape the hat and to make a pouring lip **(4)**. Paint the whole jug with white emulsion paint.
Then, paint the face and clothes **(5)**. A black rim forms the Toby's hat. When the paint is completely dry, give the jug a good finish one or two coats of clear varnish all over, including underneath.

Plastic food pots of all shapes and sizes can be modelled with pulp and paper pieces to make attractive containers. The finished pot is fairly durable and it can be used as a holder but not to contain liquid.
Very inexpensive gifts can be made with this technique. You do not necessarily have to make Toby jugs. They are very nice to have, particularly if you made a set of three in different sizes, but they might be a bit difficult for you at first. Try simpler moulded decorations, such as eyebrows, nose and a laughing mouth.
You might try making a clown pot for a desk set, to be filled with pens and pencils. Or a pretty doll-like face for a dressing table pot to be used for holding make-up pencils, tweezers etc., or for the bathroom to hold toothbrushes. For a Christmas party, make Santa Claus faces and fill the pots with sweets or biscuits.

Puppet heads
Working on a plastic pot base, model puppet heads and make holes round the rim so that the bodies can be stitched on. Glove puppets are particularly easy to make on plastic pots and there is enough space to move fingers easily.

PROJECT

Castle keep

Materials, tools and equipment
610 × 910mm (24 × 36in) sheet of hardboard, stressed with battens
Polystyrene tiles
Polystyrene tile cutter and battery
Pulp egg cartons, cardboard, string,
Clear adhesive tape
Coloured sawdust
Emulsion paint
Paints, brushes, newspaper, paste
Ruler, felt-tipped pens

Method
Castle walls and gatehouse Using the tile-cutter, cut the four walls of the gatehouse, 280mm (11in) high and 200mm (8in) wide. Cut an archway in

two of the four walls. Crenellate the tops of the walls **(1)**.

Castle walls Cut these with crenellated tops; they should be 200mm (8in) in height. Make the walls two tiles thick. Roof the keep just below the battlements with a square piece of tile. Fasten the pieces together with pasted strips of paper. Do not use ordinary glues – some adhesives melt polystyrene.

Prime the base board with emulsion paint. Form a flat-topped mound for the castle to stand on by glueing whole egg boxes to the base board **(2)**. Leave a moat before the castle walls, build up the rest of the terrain with the help of egg boxes and dry balls of newspaper **(3)**. Build up the terrain and the sides of the moat with pulp. With large sheets of paste-soaked newspaper, layer over the castle walls, the egg boxes and those parts of the terrain that require grading to form gentle slopes. Leave this to dry.

The drawbridge Cut a 76mm × 127mm (3in × 5in) piece of stout cardboard for the bridge. Hinge to the base of the castle walls at the gateway arch with tape. At the other end of the bridge, attach a 460mm (18in) length of string to one corner. Thread the string through a hole in the castle wall at the head of the arch, across behind the arch, back through another hole on the far side of the arch, and finally attach to the other corner of the drawbridge. The bridge can be raised by pulling on the string inside the keep **(4)**.

Rhino bank

This is another project where pulp and paper strips are used to alter the shape of the basic form. Depending on the shape of the form underneath, a variety of animals can be made. You might build up a whole farmyard or zoo. Legs or long necks are handled in the same way as the rhino's feet. Roll and glue tubes of paper and join them to the body with pasted strips of paper. To attach the legs, lay the body on its back, supported with two lumps of clay. The legs will balance on the body while the pasted strips dry. Position the strips so that half lies up the legs, the other half on the body.

Other ideas for bottles

Windowsill garden Cut one side of the bottle away. Fix four feet to the underside (make the feet from wound and pasted strips of paper). Screw the bottle cap on. Cover the bottle with strips of pasted paper, adding several layers at the neck to smooth out the shoulders. Pierce holes in the underside. Paint with two coats of emulsion paint and then decorate. Fill with soil and plant with small plants or succulents.

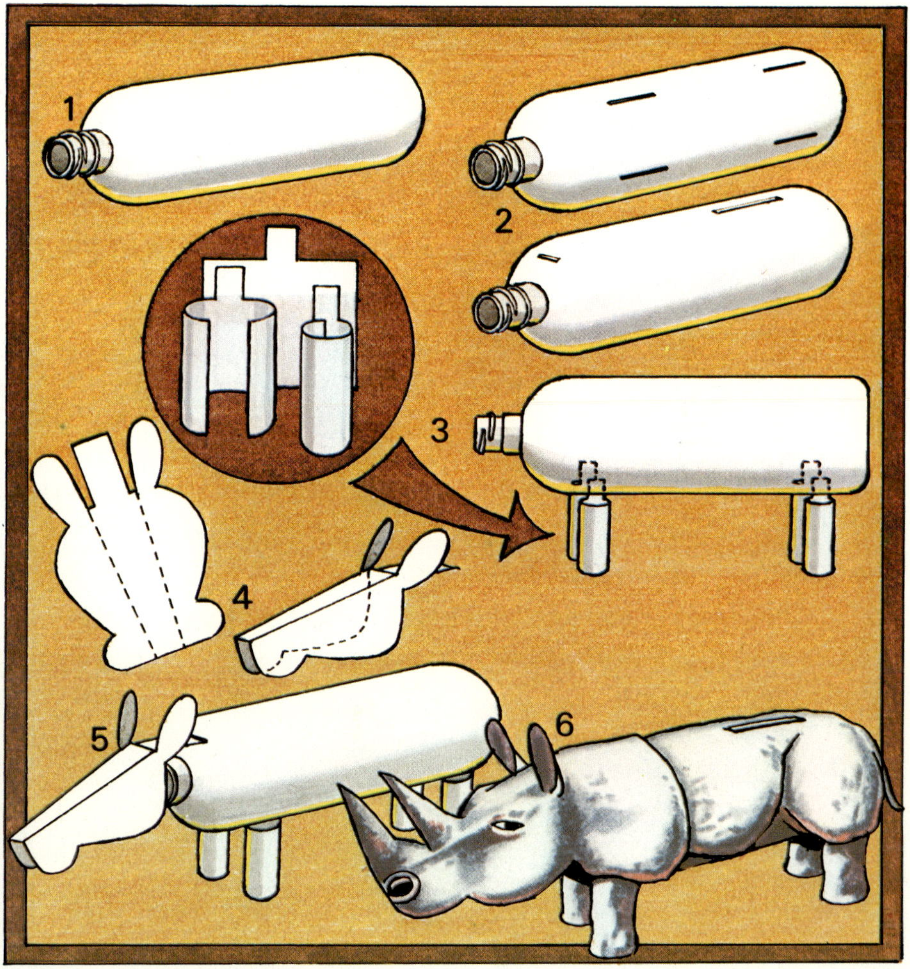

Tools, materials and equipment
Plastic detergent bottle
Thin cardboard, newspaper, paste
Crafts' knife, paints

Method
Wash out the bottle, dry it. Lay the bottle on its side **(1)**. Using the crafts' knife, cut four 25mm (1in) long slits for the legs. Cut one 12mm (½in) slit on the opposite side of the bottle at the base of the neck running crossways for head. Cut the slit to admit the money **(2)**. Make four cardboard cylinders 13mm (½in) in diameter and 38mm (1½in) long each with a tab to insert in the leg slits **(3)**. For the head, draw and cut out the shape illustrated and cut out in card. Fold along dotted lines and insert tab in the neck slit. Bend the ears forward **(4)**. Bind pasted strips of paper loosely where the legs join the body. The loose binding will result in creases just like rhinoceros skin.
For the horns, roll two cones of pasted paper and paste with strips to the rhino's nose. Use pulp to model the brows, shoulders and haunches. Layer over the entire body and head fairly loosely to promote creasing **(5)**. Paint the rhino, picking out eyes and nostrils in red **(6)**.

Monster feet

If the monster feet are going to be part of a costume, pierce holes for sewing on leggings.

Materials, tools and equipment
Stiff card for the soles, pliable, thin card for straps and claws, scissors, a pencil, adhesive
Paper pulp, strips, paste
Paints, brushes

Method
Stand barefoot on a piece of stiff card. Draw round your foot following the outline exactly **(1)**. Now draw the outline of a monster foot round this, adding a 'thumb' on the inside edge **(2)**. Cut round the monster outline.
Make two 25mm (1in) wide straps for each foot long enough to go over the foot with 25mm (1in) extra at each end for sticking to sole **(3)**. Glue the ends firmly to the sole on either side **(4)**. To make the monster toes, cut 5 pieces of card 25mm × 12mm (1in × ½in) and roll and glue to make tubes. Glue these to the sole **(5)**.
Tear strips of newspaper, dip these in the paste, and use them to link the two straps. Each strip must be pasted to both straps. In the same way join the lower strap to the toes **(6)**. Make claws by glueing cones of flexible card into the ends of the toe tubes **(7)**. Build up the tops of the feet to make them knobbly and monster-like by adding lumps of papier mâché pulp. Model bulges at the base of the claws. Layer twice over the whole foot. Leave the feet to dry overnight and then paint them **(8)**.

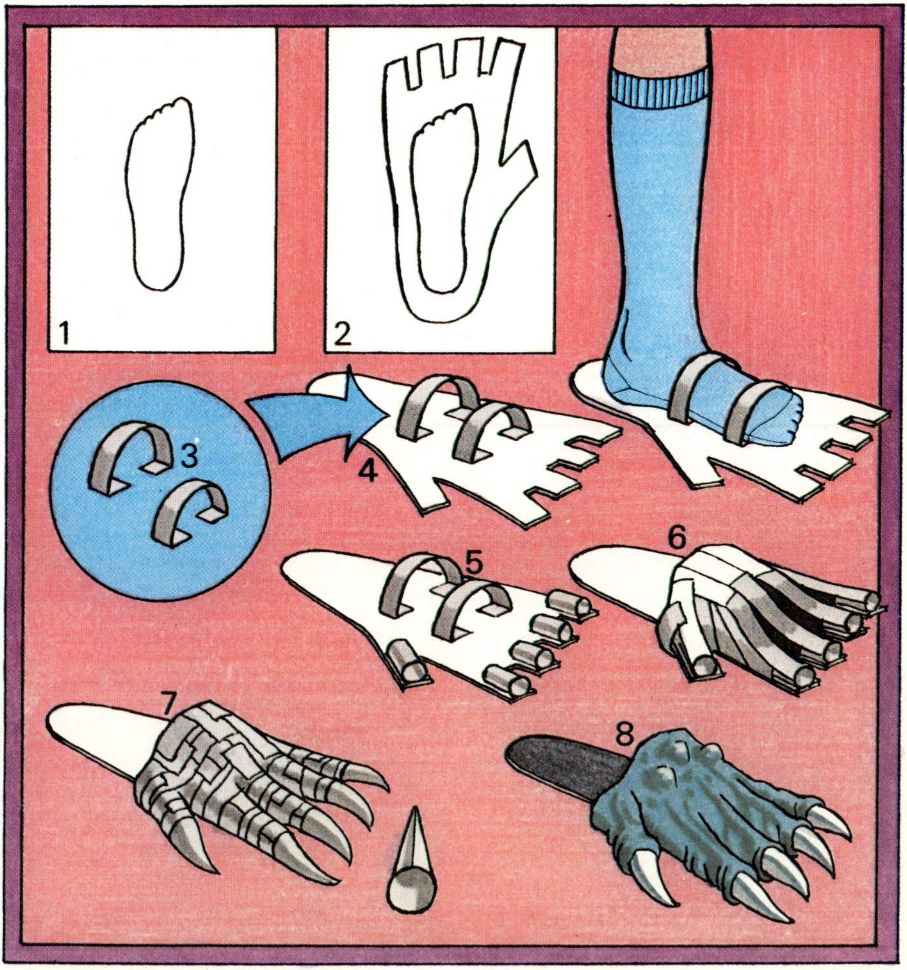

Other animal feet
Use the same technique to make feet for other carnival or pantomime animals – dragons, horses, cows etc. Do not be tempted to work over an old pair of shoes or sandals because they are likely to be too flexible. The soles must be rigid or the upper part will break off as the wearer walks. Monster feet are walked in with a kind of shuffling movement.

Monster hands
Hands for monster costumes are made in a very similar way except that the tubes for the fingers should be wide enough to be able to slip your fingers into. Hands could be made curled with talons at the ends of the fingers. You might like to glue real fur or imitation hair to the backs of your monster hands. Pierce holes round the wrists so that they can be sewn to the sleeves of the costume.

Decorating
When painting monster feet and hands, brush paint on liberally for the first coat. Add highlights and shadows by dipping a piece of cotton wool into thick poster paint and dabbing it on. Varnishing is optional. If you are using enamel paints of course, varnishing is not necessary.

PROJECT

Carnival disguise

You and your friends can have a lot of fun making carnival disguises. Start with a pair of wire spectacles, covered in layers of pasted paper and hang the rest of the disguise from the frames.

Hair and teeth

Artificial hair can be added to make bushy eyebrows. Glue it to the spectacle frames after papering. Glue a droopy moustache over the card moustache. You can even make a beard by cutting a spade shape in card first with two curved pieces joining it to the nose piece. Cover the card with cotton wool or with wool yarn cut into lengths. Big, goofy teeth are cut from white card, glued to a strip and fastened behind the moustache.

Noses and ears

You can experiment with all kinds of noses. A long, beaky nose is made from a triangular-shaped piece of card, folded and glued to the spectacles between the eyes. A droopy nose can be shaped in the same way. What about trying a pair of bright red cauliflower ears? Cut them out of card and tape them to the sides of the spectacles eye-pieces. With a wig made of fringed crêpe paper, glued to a dome made of layered papier mâché (page 35), no one could possibly recognize you.

Materials, tools and equipment

Light-weight flexible wire
A pulp egg box
Card
Adhesive tape
Newspaper, paste and paint

Method

Cut a 915mm (36in) long piece of wire. In the centre make two small hoops to form upper part of spectacle eye-pieces with a bar over bridge of nose **(1)**. Bend wire round to form ear-pieces, double it back to eye-pieces again **(2)**. Twist the wire 3 times round itself at outer edge of eye-frames, make lower frames for eye-pieces. The two ends of wire meet at the bridge of the nose. Twist together and cut off excess. Cut one cup from an egg box. Fix between eyes with tape. Cut a curly moustache shape in card. Attach below nose with tape **(3)**. Layer nose-piece to make it bulbous **(4)**. Bind spectacle frames with pasted strips **(5)**. When dry, paint the nose bright pink and the frames and moustache black **(6)**.

Jewellery tree

The jewellery tree is a good project on which to practise making armatures. It is easy to do and making something simple will help you to get used to handling wire. Sculptors use wire armatures when they are building their clay machettes (first miniature models) so this is a useful technique to learn if you like modelling.

Decide on the finished height of the little tree. Remember that you will be bending about one third out for the base. When you are adding branches, leave a long end to wind round the main branch to thicken it. Bend the branch ends up slightly so that rings do not drop off.

Decorating trees

Make little trees for table decorations for parties. Paint the branches white, gold or silver. Spread glue on them and sprinkle glitter dust. Wire tiny glass baubles to the ends of the branches. For a summer party, make tiny flowers

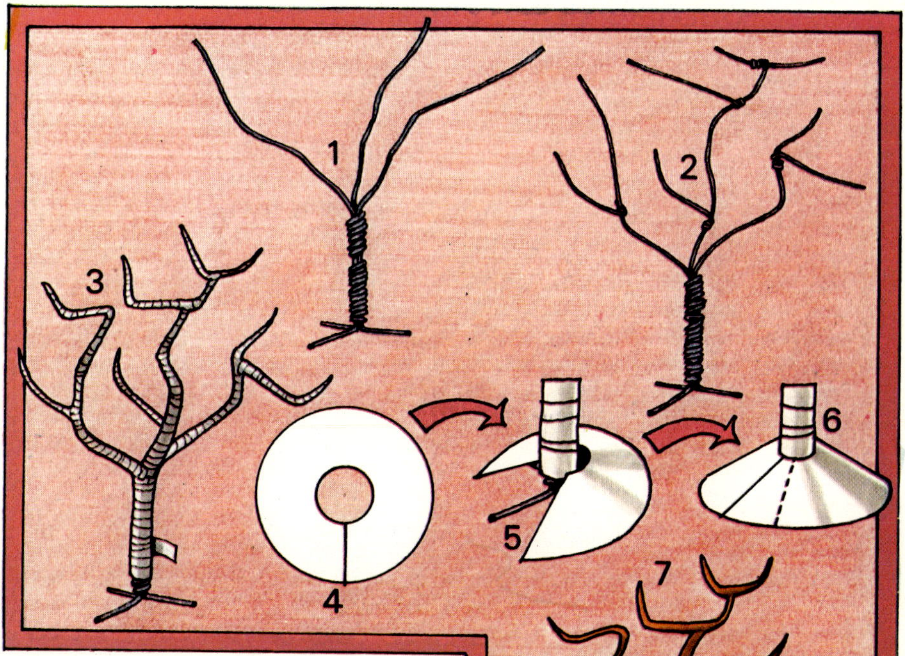

from tissue paper. Cut strips, pleat them and then double them over. Wind fusewire round the fold and separate the pleats to make flowers. Wire the flowers all over a tree painted in a pastel colour.

Model trees Little trees made in this way look pretty in models of farms or castles. Make foliage by soaking balls of cotton wool or tissue paper in thick, green poster paint. Leave the balls to dry and glue to the branches.

Materials, tools and equipment
Medium-weight flexible wire
Thin card, newspaper, paste, paint

Method
Cut the wire into three equal lengths. Twist 3 strands together to form the trunk of the tree. Splay the ends out to make a base and so that the tree stands up **(1)**. Splay out the other end for branches. Make extra branches by cutting small pieces of wire and twisting them onto the main branches **(2)**. Bind the trunk and branches with strips of pasted paper. The trunk should be the thickest part of the tree and the branches should taper. Do not bind the base wires **(3)**. Cut a disc of card. Cut a hole in the centre to fit the trunk. Cut along a line from the centre to the rim **(4)**. Slide the trunk of the tree through the cut to the centre of the disc **(5)**. Overlap the two cut edges so that the disc makes a shallow cone to support the tree and cover the wire base **(6)**. Paint the tree and the base and stand it on your dressing table **(7)**.

Angel fish mobile

The next stage is making armatures for three-dimensional shapes. These fish are made on a simple armature structure and by the time you have made five or six for a mobile you will feel quite confident about tackling something larger.

Making a mobile
Arrange something to hang the mobile from while you are working on it. A piece of string tied from one side of the room to the other will do. Cut the first bar from rigid wire. Bend the ends up slightly. Tie a piece of strong thread to the middle and hang it from the string. It should hang level. Move the knot if it does not. Take a small piece of modelling clay, squeeze it onto one end of the bar. Take a prepared fish and tie a loop on the end of its thread. Slide the loop onto the bar. Move the fish along until it is balanced by the clay. Prepare another bar with a fish on each end. (Remember to bend the ends upwards.) Tie a piece of thread to the middle of the bar. Slip the loop end of a fish over the bar and then remove the clay. Move the loop along until the mobile balances. Continue adding single fish and fish on bars, using clay bits for a balance until the mobile is completed. The fish should all hang at different levels **(7)**.
Do not have mobiles hanging below head level or someone will get their eyes and mouth full of fish while rushing to answer the telephone!

Materials, tools and equipment
Flexible, medium weight wire
Cotton thread
Clear adhesive tape
Rigid wire for mobile arms
Newspaper, paste and paint

Method
To make one fish, cut a piece of wire about 76cm (30in) long. Begin by making one of the streamers, bend the wire round for the head and go on to make the upper fin. Bend the wire down to form the triangle of the tail. Carry on to make the lower fin and finish with the second streamer **(1)**. Give the tail one complete twist **(2)**. Lay the wire shape on the table. Crumple paste-soaked newspaper to form the thickness of the body. Arrange it inside the wire shape **(3)**. Paste strips of pasted paper over the pulp, to the wire and over the edge **(4)**. Turn fish over and layer the other side. Leave it to dry, then layer all over with very fine pieces of paper. Remember to keep the fins and tail thin, though the body should bulge. Make a hole in the fish for hanging **(5)**. Thread cotton through the hole. Tie a knot. Note whether the fish hangs evenly. Make another hole if necessary to make sure that it does. Cut pieces of rigid wire for mobile arms. Bend ends upwards. Tie fish to arms **(6)**.

Dinosaur model

The armature for making a dinosaur model is a little more complex. Make the outline shape first and if it is correct you will find that the later shaping with paper strips is easy. The legs are made in pairs and attached separately. Make sure that the legs are the correct length so that the body stands steadily.

If you are making another kind of dinosaur, such as a tyrannosaurus, the creature had a thick tail and very small front legs. The tail and big hind legs must be constructed so that they balance the body. It will help you at the layering stage if the tail and neck have rings of wire fixed up the length. It is difficult to push balls of paper into these spaces so mix a little paper pulp and use this instead.

Making monster models

Work your models to scale if possible. Find accurate pictures or drawings and work from these. After the model has been finished and realistically painted, you might like to try making a set for it. Obtain a large cardboard box and cut away 2 sides. Paint the outside. Build rocks, jungly growth etc., with paper pulp and strips. Paint the inside of the box to look like a prehistoric landscape. Sprinkle sand on the bottom and stand your monster in the box.

Method

Cut a piece of wire about 760mm (30in) long – one end is the base of neck **(1)**. Take wire up and make a loop for head, twist loop to make neck. Bend back down along neck, up to humped back and down to tail. Bend wire back on itself and twist end round to make tail stiff. Bend for underbody and up to base of neck again. Trim wire end off, twist ends together round base of neck **(2)**. **Front legs** Cut wire about 510mm (20in) long. Twist first foot about along length. Leave a short end. Take the other end up to the backbone, twist round and down to make second foot. Twist foot and join the short ends of both feet to underbody. **Back legs** Twist a foot first like front legs **(3)**. Then take wire up and around backbone to make second leg. Make leg, twist both ends of wire round underbody wire for stability. Screw up some 50mm (2in) balls of dry newspaper, stuff the body cavity **(4)**. Bind the model with pasted strips. Leave to dry. Continue binding with pasted paper until legs, neck etc. are the right thickness. Twist paper to make tendons and muscles, paste onto the body. Finish with small pieces of paper for a smooth surface **(5)**. Paint and decorate **(6)**.

Model soldier

With this technique you will be able to make model figures of all kinds.

Materials, tools and equipment
A piece of board for the base
Two 25mm (1in) nails, hammer
Thick and thin flexible wire
Card, adhesive tape
Newspaper, paste, paint

Method
Hammer two nails into the base board with about half protruding above the board. The nails should be 76mm (3in) apart. Cut a piece of thick wire about 46cm (18in) long for the legs. Wind one end of the wire tightly round one of the nails. Take the wire straight up for 150mm (6in), then bend it across horizontally for 48mm (1½in) then down to the other nail. Wind it round as before. Use the wire ends to give extra stability to the legs by bracing them against the board **(1)**. For the rest of the armature use thin wire. Cut a piece 36cm (14in) long to frame the body and shoulders

(2). Form the head and spine with a piece of wire twisted first round the 'hips' strand and then round the 'shoulders'. To make the arms, twist the hand loop on one end, take it up to the shoulder, twist once then down to the spine, up to the other shoulder and make the second arm and hand **(3)**. Bend the body and limbs into the stance required. Crumble a ball of dry newspaper and push this into the head loop of wire. Build up the shoulders and trunk with paste-soaked pulp. Build up the arms and legs by binding with paste-dipped strips. Layer over the pulp and the head **(4)**. Leave to dry. Make a card cylinder of about 25mm (1in) diameter to fit over the head as the hat. Cut a peak for the hat out of card and glue it in place. Cut the stock of the musket from card and bind this to a straight piece of wire (for the barrel) with tape. Attach the hat to the head and the gun to the hands with adhesive tape. Layer the gun and the hat with small pieces of paper **(5)**.

To make the webbing straps, fold paste-soaked strips of paper into three and paste them across the chest and back. Use the same technique for the collar and cuffs **(6)**. Finer details can now be modelled with pulped tissue paper. When everything is dry, paint the model with emulsion paint first, then paint with enamel paint. Paint the base **(7)**.

Dragon's head

This project uses the basic principle of making armatures for human figures. The dragon's head has a jaw which can be moved from inside by the wearer.

Materials, tools and equipment
Thick and thin wire, pliers
Newspaper, paste and paints

Method
Cut a piece of thick wire and bend it into an elongated pear-shape **(1)**. Lay this down horizontally and take the wire up to form the nose and crown of the dragon **(2)**. Secure the far end of the wire by twisting it round the horizontal wire at the back of the neck **(3)**. This frame must be large enough to fit over your head easily so try it on to check. Twist additional hoops of fine wire crossways over the snout and head of the dragon to give added rigidity. Make extra loops in the foremost hoop to form the nostrils. Make an extra long hoop above the eyes to form a frame for the jutting brow, and a shallower inner hoop to rest against your forehead **(4)**. Twist on two loops of thick wire at the base of the jaw. This will be hinged with similar loops on the lower jaw. For the lower jaw, cut a length of wire. Thread the ends through the hinge loops on the upper jaw and twist round into a loop. These should be large, loose loops so that the hinge will move easily. Attach a U-shaped piece of wire at the base of

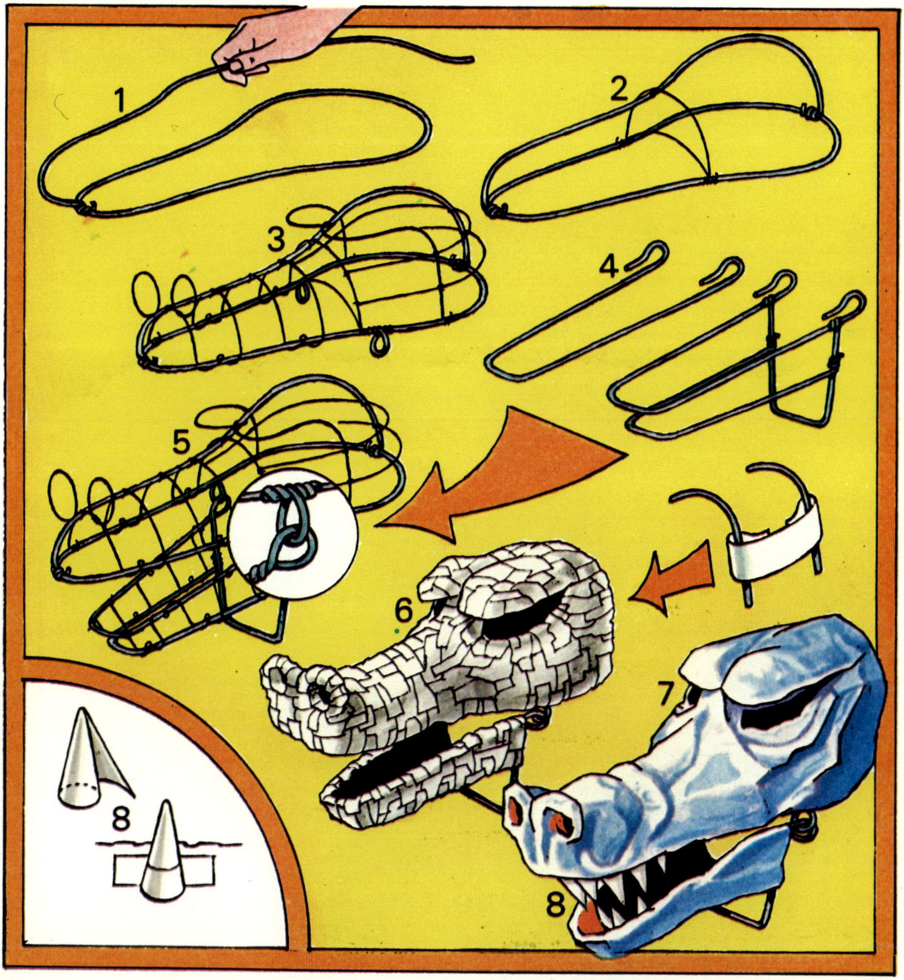

the hinge. This will form a handle so that you can open and close the dragon's mouth. Add a second horizontal wire below the lower jaw by twisting the end around the handle. Using fine wire, twist ribbing to join the upper and lower wires together and hold them rigid **(5)**.

Layering Layer along the ribbing. Since pasted paper will not stick to wire, you will have to loop each strip of paper round a wire rib and stick it to itself. The other end of the strip is looped round an opposite rib so that the paper is held taut **(6)**.

Layer all over the head with pasted strips. Mould the brow and nostrils and wrinkles around the eyes and along the nose with paper pulp **(7)**. Leaving openings for the eyes, layer over the entire structure with three or four layers of papier mâché. The back of the head needs to be extra strong so add another layer here. Make sure the dragon's lips are thick and well layered.

Make cones of pasted paper for the teeth and attach them to the inside of the jaw with strips of pasted paper. Layer over them again for strength **(8)**. When the mask is thoroughly dry it can be painted. The handle allows the wearer to open and shut the dragon mask mouth while it is being worn.

Stage armour

Wire mesh enables you to form large lightweight shapes which can be covered with paper. Armour for theatrical productions – breastplates, shields, helmets, etc. – is just one of the things that can be made. Big carnival heads of beasts and mythical monsters are made in the same way. Working over wire mesh is quicker than working over a wooden frame and the resulting head is far more comfortable to wear. The technique can be used to make movable scenery for plays and pageants. Rocks, boulders, grassy banks, cave mouths, rough stone fireplaces – big shapes such as these are first shaped in wire mesh and then papered over. If a rock or bank is going to be used as a seat, mould the wire over a stool or bench. Stage props made in this way are easily shifted by stage hands.

Materials, tools and equipment

Wire mesh and wire cutters
String or tape
Cardboard
Newspaper and paste
Gold spray paint
Black emulsion paint, brush

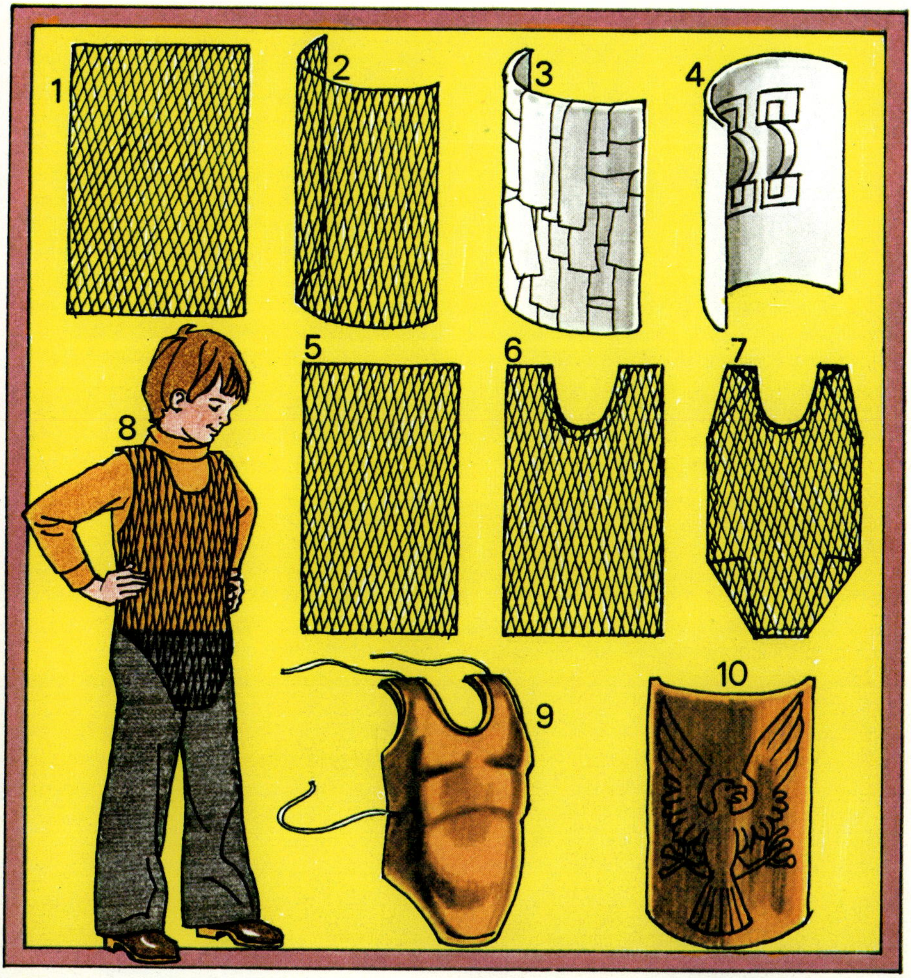

Method

Shield Using the wire cutters, cut a 61cm × 91cm (2ft × 3ft) rectangle of wire mesh **(1)**. Fold over the jagged edges of the wire to protect your hands. Holding the shield upright, gently bend the mesh so it forms a shallow curve **(2)**. Now start layering with fairly large pieces of newspaper. The paste will not stick to the mesh so you must press the outside layer and inside layer towards each other so that they meet through the mesh. Three or four layers should produce a smooth surface and get rid of the honeycomb pattern of the mesh. Layer over the edges **(3)**. Make two 38mm (1½in) straps from thick cardboard. Stick them to the inside of the shield with adhesive and layer over the join for strength **(4)**. Spray gold.

Breastplate Cut a rectangle of mesh large enough to protect the trunk of your body with a little to spare **(5)**. Cut away a U-shape for the neck **(6)**. Fold the mesh inwards to form the shoulder pieces, and below the waist fold the mesh so that the breast-plate tapers towards a point. Fold over all raw edges **(7)**.

Hold the breast plate against you and press it against your body to fit **(8)**.

Attach string at shoulders and sides of the breast plate at waist level **(9)**.

Layer, building up the chest slightly with slabs of pulp. Spray gold **(10)**.

Helmet for stage armour

Helmet to wear with the breastplate.

Materials, tools and equipment
Wire mesh 455 × 610mm (18 × 24in)
Wire cutters, chalk
Newspaper and paste
Black emulsion paint
Card, scissors
Clear adhesive
Gold spray paint

Method
Form a cylinder of mesh 455mm (18in) high and of a diameter which will allow you to pass it over your head and face without grazing. Overlap the edges and snip off any sharp ends of metal. The lower edge should be at chin level **(1)**. Crush down the top part of the cylinder to form the crown of the helmet **(2)**. Whilst the cylinder is still on your head, mark the face opening with chalk. Take off the helmet and cut the opening **(3)**. Gently ease open the inside of the helmet with your hands to allow room for layering. Fold over the raw edges and bend outwards the lower edge of the helmet to make the neck-guard **(4)**. Layer with fairly large pieces of paper. The first layer is worked on both the inside and outside at the same time, pressing the layers together through the mesh. Layer until the wire cannot be seen through the paper **(5)**. Cut three pieces of card 185mm (7in) long, 50mm (2in), 37mm (1½in) and 25mm (1in) wide. Curve each to fit the top of the helmet. Glue on the widest first then the narrow strips **(6)**.

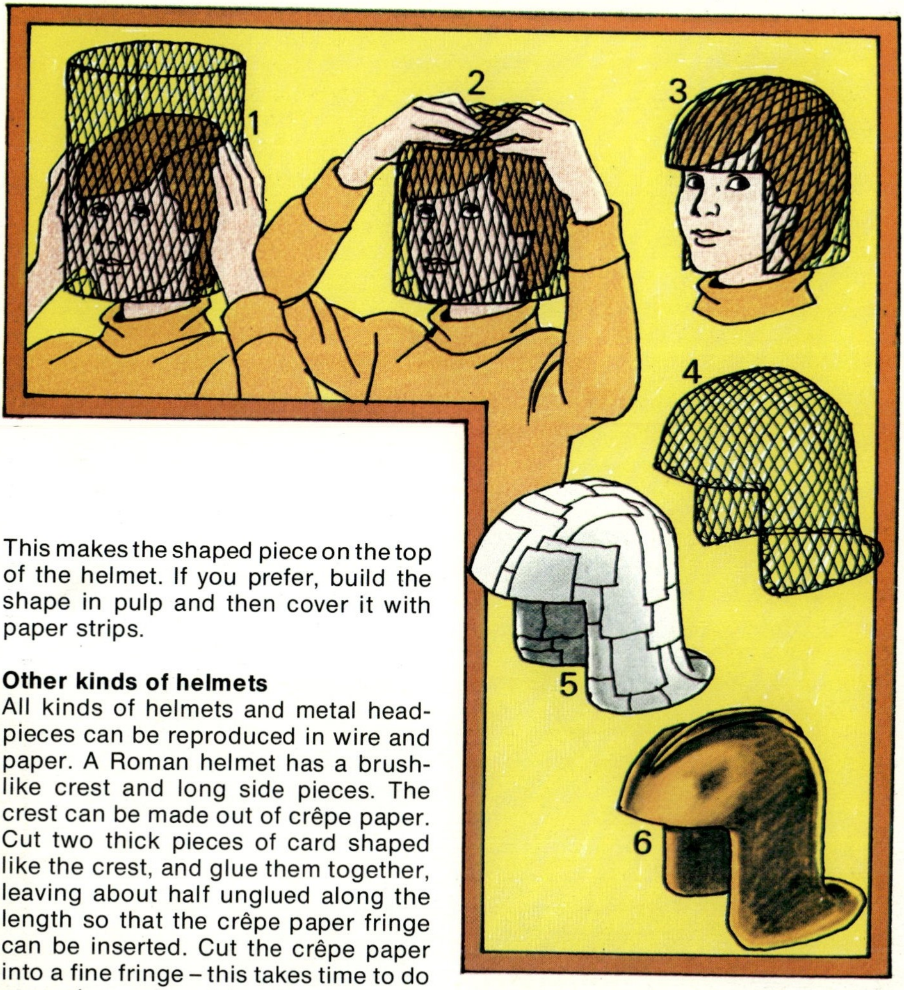

This makes the shaped piece on the top of the helmet. If you prefer, build the shape in pulp and then cover it with paper strips.

Other kinds of helmets
All kinds of helmets and metal head-pieces can be reproduced in wire and paper. A Roman helmet has a brush-like crest and long side pieces. The crest can be made out of crêpe paper. Cut two thick pieces of card shaped like the crest, and glue them together, leaving about half unglued along the length so that the crêpe paper fringe can be inserted. Cut the crêpe paper into a fine fringe – this takes time to do properly – and push into the card crest with the help of a knife blade. Trim the fringe to shape it. Spray the helmet and the fringed crest with gold paint.

Painting Paint armour with black emulsion paint first. Then spray gold or silver spray paint to give an antique finish. When this is dry, paint a heraldic device on your shield and breastplate in black.

Tips on painting
For spraying gold or silver paint onto a model, first prime it in black or grey emulsion paint and then spread news-paper over a large area. Stand your model in the centre of the paper to spray it as some of the spray is bound to miss the model. If you wish to give a particularly hard waterproof finish to your model, you may varnish it. Any clear varnish may be used so long as it is designed for indoor use. Some var-nishes are slow to harden, taking up to twenty-four hours. Art shops sell a quick-drying variety. If you apply two coats of varnish be sure to allow the first to harden completely before apply-ing the second or both may peel off together! It is best to varnish in a well ventilated room. The fumes can make you unwell.

Useful addresses

Crafts materials	Hobby Horse Langton Street London SW10
Adhesives, adhesive tape Paper, card,	W.H. Smith & Son (larger branches)
Paints, brushes, artist's materials, non-bake clay, craft's knives Gesso powder	Reeves & Son 13 Charing Cross Road London WC2
Emulsion paints	F.W. Woolworth & Co. Ltd (most branches)
Polystyrene tile cutters, pliers, wire cutters, wire	General ironmonger's shops
Oil of wintergreen	Boots Chemists (most branches)